Making Sense

HODDER
EDUCATION
AN HACHETTE UK COMPANY

The publishers would like to thank the following for permission to reproduce copyright material:

Photo credits: page 1 © mirpic – Fotolia; page 2 *t*, © Imagestate Media (John Foxx); page 2 *c, l* © Pictorius – Fotolia; page 2 *c, r* © CSeigneurgens – Fotolia.com; page 2 *b, r* © Andrew Skinner – Fotolia; page 6 *t* © Steve Gough; page 14 © Kate Crossland-Page; page 15 *all photos* © Steve Gough; page 20 *t* © Denis Dryashkin – Fotolia; page 21 © Kate Crossland-Page; pages 28 – 34 *all photos* © Frank Eade; page 37 © CUKMEN – Fotolia; pages 38 – 39 *all photos* © Paul Dickinson; page 41 © Kate Crossland-Page; page 42 © Paul Dickinson; page 43 *all photos* © Kate Crossland-Page; page 46 © Aleksey Bakaleev – Fotolia; page 48 *l* © Kate Crossland-Page; page 48 *r* © Anne Wanjie; page 49 *t, l* © Galyna Andrushko – Fotolia; page 49 *t, r* and *c* and *b* © Sue Hough; page 54 *all photos* © Sue Hough; pages 60 – 61 *all photos* © Sue Hough; pages 64 – 65 *all photos* © Sue Hough; page 66 *t* © Sue Hough; page 66 *b, l* © Ingram Publishing Limited; page 66 *b, r* © Sue Hough; page 67 *all photos* © Sue Hough; page 71 *b* © kovaleff – Fotolia; page 72 © Mopic – Fotolia; page 73 © Justin Kase zninez / Alamy; page 74 © Steve Gough; page 78 *t* © Happy Arts – Fotolia; page 78 *b* © Steve Gough; page 79 *all photos* © Steve Gough; page 80 *t* © Sue Hough; page 80 *b, r* and *b, l* © Kate Crossland-Page; page 81 © Steve Gough

t = top, *c* = centre, *b* = bottom, *l* = left, *r* = right

All designated trademarks and brands are protected by their respective trademarks.

Every effort has been made to trace all copyright holders, but if any have been inadvertently overlooked, the Publishers will be pleased to make the necessary arrangements at the first opportunity.

Although every effort has been made to ensure that website addresses are correct at time of going to press, Hodder Education cannot be held responsible for the content of any website mentioned in this book. It is sometimes possible to find a relocated web page by typing in the address of the home page for a website in the URL window of your browser.

Hachette UK's policy is to use papers that are natural, renewable and recyclable products and made from wood grown in sustainable forests. The logging and manufacturing processes are expected to conform to the environmental regulations of the country of origin.

Orders: please contact Bookpoint Ltd, 130 Milton Park, Abingdon, Oxon OX14 4SB. Telephone: (44) 01235 827720. Fax: (44) 01235 400454. Lines are open 9.00–5.00, Monday to Saturday, with a 24-hour message answering service. Visit our website at www.hoddereducation.co.uk

© Paul Dickinson, Stella Dudzic, Frank Eade, Steve Gough, Sue Hough 2012

First published in 2012 by
Hodder Education, a Hachette UK company,
338 Euston Road
London NW1 3BH

Impression number 5 4 3 2 1
Year 2016 2015 2014 2013 2012

Cover photo © Sue Hough
Illustrations by Integra Software Services Ltd
Typeset in India by Integra Software Services Ltd
Printed in Spain

A catalogue record for this title is available from the British Library

ISBN 978 1444 180107

Contents

Introduction   v

Chapter 1: Whole numbers

- A new computer game   1
- Historical events   2
- Jumps on a number line   4
- How many?   6
- Multiplications   8
- Divisions   10
- Buying ribbon   11
- Buying tickets   15
- The rules for calculations   16
- Summary   17

Chapter 2: Measure for measure

- Measuring instruments   19
- Ten thousand steps a day   20
- Height   21
- Motorway routes   24
- A real bargain?   25
- Watch your speed!   28
- Weighing it up   31
- Rounding   35
- Summary   36

Chapter 3: Using ratio tables

- Recipes   37
- Fuel consumption   42
- Speed   44
- Mobile phone density   46
- Summary   48

Chapter 4: The positives and the negatives

■ The highs and lows on Earth   49

■ Time is moving along   52

■ The witch's cauldron   54

■ Summary   60

Chapter 5: The building blocks of numbers

■ A numbers game   61

■ Using primes to build other numbers   62

■ Playing out   64

■ Packing boxes   67

■ Finding the highest common factor   68

■ Finding the lowest common multiple   69

■ Summary   70

Chapter 6: Big numbers

■ Writing big numbers   71

■ Writing mathematically – power notation   72

■ Big cities?   73

■ A strange reward?   74

■ Problems with tiling   78

■ A special power   80

■ Summary   82

Introduction

These books are intended to help you to make sense of the maths you do in school and the maths you need to use outside school. They have already been tried out in classrooms, and are the result of many comments made by the teachers and the students who have used them. Students told us that after working with these materials they were more able to understand the maths they had done, and teachers found that students also did better in tests and examinations.

Most of the time you will be working 'in context' – in other words, in real-life situations that you will either have been in yourself or can imagine being in. For example, in this book you will be looking at preparing for a wedding, journeying to France, using recipes and tiling, among many other things.

You will regularly be asked to 'draw something' – drawings and sketches are very important in maths and often help us to solve problems and to see connections between different topics. In the trials, students found that drawing a number bar or a ratio table helped them to develop an understanding of how to solve many problems in number.

You will also be expected to talk about your maths, explaining your ideas to small groups or to the whole class. We all learn by explaining our own ideas and by listening to and trying out the ideas of others.

Finally, of course, you will be expected to practice solving problems and answering examination questions.

We hope that through working in this way you will come to understand the maths you do, enjoy examination success, and be confident when using your maths outside school.

A new computer game

1 Aisha is desperate to be one of the first to own a new computer game. She knows that the game is going to be popular so she gets to the shop before it opens. There is a very, very long queue. The shop gives everyone a ticket with their position in the queue so no one can push in. Aisha has number 743.

Draw a sketch of the queue showing Aisha's position.

2 Aisha sends a text to all her friends, who are also in the queue: Im 743 wot # R u?

These are the responses:

Jack	Im #1232
Laura	Im clOs jst 53 plAcz n frnt of U
Hannah	Im near d nd, #1537
Mohammad	LckE I wz earlE #54
Callum	988
Mariam	520 Bhind U

a) What is Laura's number?

b) What is Mariam's number?

c) Find the difference between Aisha's number and the numbers of each of her friends. Use number lines like the one below.

743

Historical events

3 Below you will see some different historical events.

21 July 1969

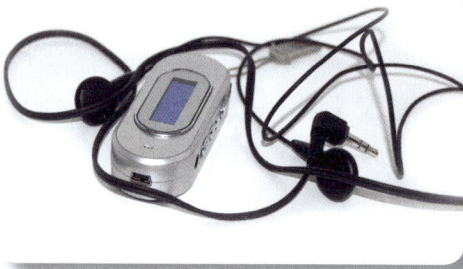

An early MP3 player (1998)

An early version of the iPod (2001)

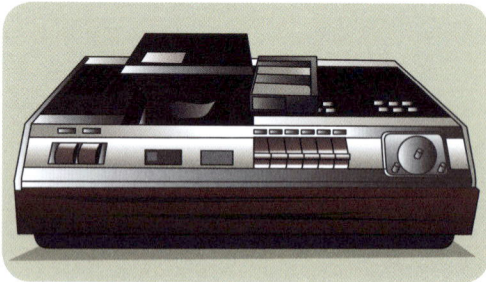

The first video cassette recorder
(VCR) was sold in 1971

The Millennium Dome

WWW

In 1991 the World Wide Web was released to the public.

Copy the number line below and place the events on the number line.

2000

4 Use the number line from **question 3** to answer the following questions.

 a) How many years after the launch of the first MP3 player was the first iPod produced?

 b) How many years ago was the World Wide Web released to the public?

 c) How many years ago did a man first land on the Moon?

5 **a)** As a class, make your own history line. Mark on your history line six important events (these could be during your lifetime or from further back in history).

 b) Make up three questions about your history line, like the ones in **question 4**. Ask another student to answer your questions.

Jumps on a number line

6 Carrie, Jordan and Mich are trying to work out how many years it is from 1958 to 1975. Carrie says: 'I know how to do that. I start with a number line like this:'

'And then my next step is this...'

Below you can see what Carrie showed the others. For each step, write down what she might have said.

a)

b)

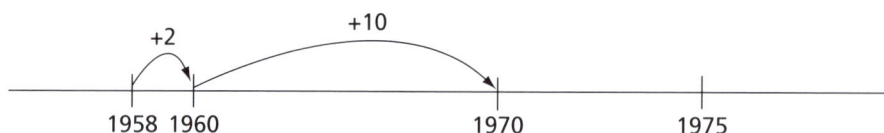

c)

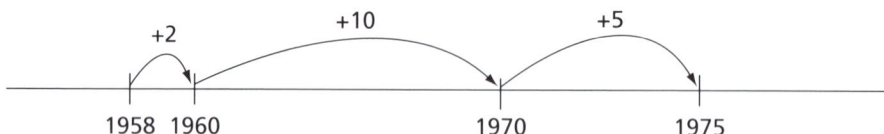

d) How many years are there from 1958 to 1975?

7 Jordan says: 'I would do it in a different way.' He shows his jumps on his number line:

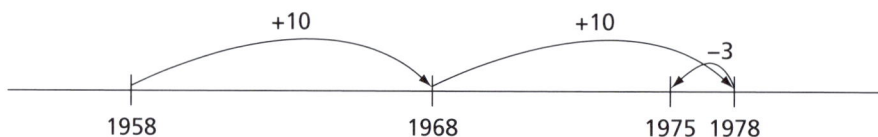

a) What was Jordan's last jump on his number line?

b) Will he find the same answer as Carrie did? Explain your answer.

8 Mich suddenly gets an idea. He says: 'The number of years from 1958 to 1975 is the same as the number of years from 1960 to 1977.'

Use the number line below to show that his idea is correct.

```
————————+—————————————————————+————————
        1958                  1975
```

> Turn to page 1 of your workbook and complete Workbook exercise 1.1. Compare your answers to those of your classmates. What did you do in the same way? What did you do differently?

9 In maths lessons you will often have seen questions like: 826 – 489 =
   a) Work out the answer to this question. Compare your method with the methods used by your classmates.
   b) How can you be sure that your answer is correct?

10 Rebecca says: 'You can use a number line to work out problems like this, where you need to find the difference between 826 and 489.'

```
————————+—————————————————————+————————
        489                   826
```

   a) Use the number line above to find the answer to 826 – 489.
   b) Use the number line in a different way to work out the same problem.

11 Work out the answers to the following questions, showing your method.
   a) 193 – 98
   b) 57 – 19
   c) 971 – 48
   d) 3000 – 1998

How many?

12 Find a way to estimate the number of people shown in the photograph above without counting them all one by one. Show your working.

13 Vanessa's mother is decorating her bathroom. She has bought 24 square mirror tiles. Four of them are shown on the right. She wants to glue them onto the wall to make a mirror but isn't sure what shape would look best.

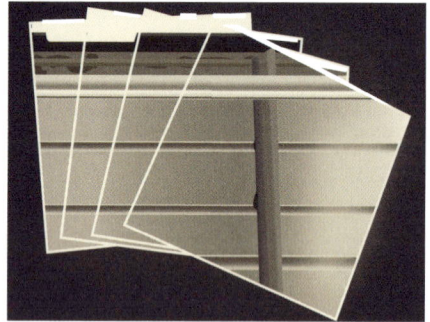

Vanessa thinks a rectangle would look good. She needs to decide which shape of rectangle would look best.

  a) Find all possible rectangles that can be made out of 24 mirror tiles.

  b) Which one do you like best for the bathroom?

14 What are all the possible rectangles that could be made from 36 tiles?

15 Vanessa wants some new tiles for the wall above the sink. The tiles on the right will be placed in the middle. The rest of the wall will be covered in white tiles.

How many tiles make up this decorated part?

16 To find out how many white tiles she needs, Vanessa draws a sketch of the wall. She calculates the total number of tiles that would fit in the width and the height.

This is what she wrote on a piece of paper:

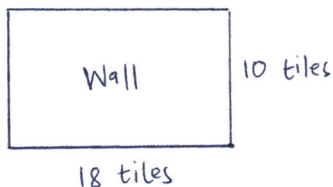

How many tiles does she need altogether? How many will be white tiles?

Turn to pages 2–3 of your workbook and try Workbook exercise 1.2. Compare your answers to those of a classmate. Write down (or draw) any differences.

17 The grid below is the plan for a tiled wall. On a copy of this plan, or using tracing paper, find two different ways to count the number of tiles needed.

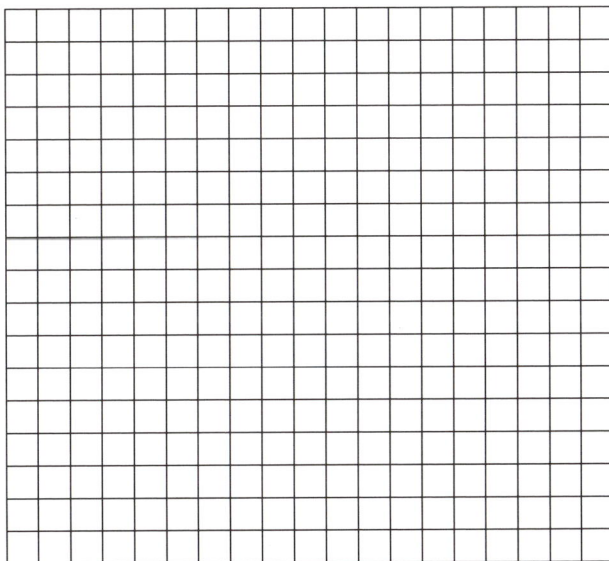

18 a) Draw a rectangular wall 17 tiles across and 14 tiles up. Find a way to count the tiles by splitting the wall up.

b) Draw the wall again and split it in a different way to help you find the number of tiles.

c) What do you think is the easiest way to split up the rectangle?

d) How is this problem similar to the tile problems in **Workbook exercise 1.2**?

Multiplications

19 If you have to multiply two numbers, you can use the idea from the previous questions (draw a rectangle and think about finding the number of tiles).

a) Make a copy of the drawing below and then calculate 25 × 24.

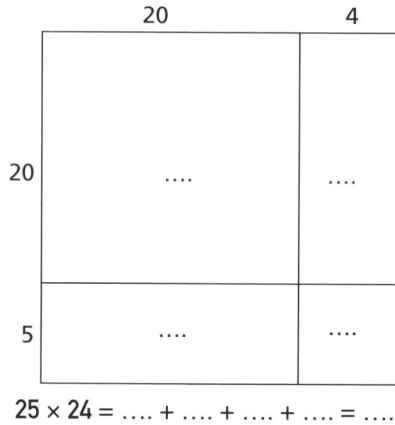

	20	4
20	….	….
5	….	….

25×24 = …. + …. + …. + …. = ….

b) Think of a tiled wall and make a drawing to show that the following is true:

$16 \times 21 = (10 \times 20) + (10 \times 1) + (6 \times 20) + (6 \times 1)$

Turn to page 4 of your workbook and complete Workbook exercise 1.3. Compare your answers and drawings with those of a classmate.

20 A lemon drink is sold in packs of six cans. Last week Woodhill Sports Club had 39 packs in stock to sell in the canteen. There are different ways to find the number of cans in 39 packs.

a) Describe a way to estimate the answer.

b) Adjust your estimate to find an exact answer.

21 Another way to find an exact answer is to use a ratio table:

Packs	1	10	20	40	39
Cans	6	60	120	240	234

a) Look at the picture and the table above and write down three statements you know to be true about the cans and packs.

b) Explain how you know each statement is true. You may use a drawing if you wish.

22 Think about how you used the ratio table in **question 21**.

a) Explain each entry in the ratio table.

b) Explain how you can work out each column from the previous column.

Turn to page 5 of your workbook and complete the problems in Workbook exercise 1.4. Compare your answers with those of a classmate. Write down (or draw) any differences.

23 Susan and Brett are discussing ratio tables. Who do you agree with, Susan or Brett? Give an example to support your choice.

With a ratio table, there is only one way to find a correct solution, so everyone has the same ratio table in the end.

There are different ways to reach the same answer with a ratio table.

Divisions

24 The canteen at Woodhill Sports Club also sells Crunchie bars. They come in cases of 24. The canteen records show that each year about 6000 Crunchie bars are sold. How many cases of Crunchie bars is this?

Write down the calculations you use to solve this problem. Compare your work with that of your classmates.

25 Bobbie found the answer using a ratio table. This is what she wrote down:

Cases	1	100	200	50	250
Crunchies	24	2400	4800	1200	6000

a) Where in this ratio table is the solution to the problem?

b) Review this ratio table solution and explain each entry.

c) Compare your own method to the ratio table method. Give two differences and two similarities between the two methods.

Turn to pages 6–7 of your workbook and complete the problems in Workbook exercise 1.5. Discuss the methods used with the rest of your class.

Buying ribbon

26 Sadie is getting married. She needs to buy some ribbon for her dress. The ribbon she wants is quite expensive. It costs £4.80 for 6 m of ribbon.

  a) Draw something to show that the cost of 6 m is £4.80.

  b) Compare your drawing with those of other members of your class.

  c) What else do you know? (Try to fill in five more amounts on your drawing.)

27 Sadie sees some other ribbon in the shop that seems less expensive. The cost of this ribbon is £2.40 for 4 m.

  a) Draw something to show that the cost of 4 m is £2.40.

  b) Try to fill in some more amounts on your drawing.

  c) Is Sadie right to think this ribbon is cheaper?

28 Sadie needs 50 m of ribbon altogether. To work out the cost of the expensive ribbon in **question 26** (£4.80 for 6 m) she draws this:

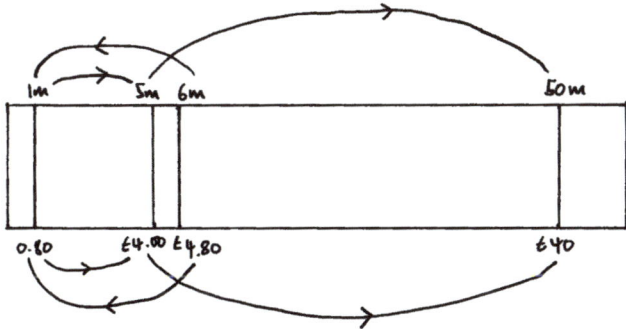

  a) Sadie started by finding the cost of 1 m of ribbon. Explain where on the diagram she found this.

  b) She then worked out the cost of 5 m of ribbon. Again, explain where on the diagram she found this.

  c) Finally, she worked out the cost of 50 m of ribbon. How did she do this?

  d) Under her drawing, she wrote this:

$$1 \times 0.8 = 0.80$$

$$5 \times 0.8 = 4.00$$

$$50 \times 0.8 = 40.00$$

Explain why she wrote down these calculations.

29 Sadie's bridesmaid, Isabella, did the calculation in a different way. She said: 'I could see from your drawing that 1 m costs £0.80. I knew I needed the cost of 50 m so I wanted to work out 50 × 0.80. So I did:

$5 \times 8 = 40$

$50 \times 8 = 400$

$50 \times 0.80 = 40$'

a) Why do you think she started with $5 \times 8 = 40$ when she wanted to find 50×0.80?

b) Explain what Isabella has done.

30 Isabella says she can use the same method to work out the cost of the less expensive ribbon (£2.40 for 4 m).

a) She says working out the cost of 1 m is easy. She draws this:

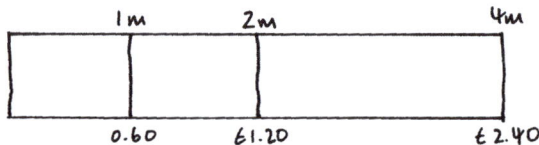

Explain how Isabella worked out the cost of 1 m.

b) She now wants to work out the cost of 50 m. This means she wants to know the answer to 50×0.60. She says:

$5 \times 6 = 30$

$50 \times 6 = 300$

$50 \times 0.60 = 30$

Explain what Isabella has done.

31 Isabella says she can use her method to work out the cost of 120 serviettes at £0.07 each. She starts by saying that $12 \times 7 = 84$. Continue with her calculation until you find the answer to 120×0.07.

32 Sadie wants to know the area of the top of her wedding cake so she knows how much icing to buy. The cake is rectangular and measures 31.2 cm by 42.3 cm.

Isabella says: 'This is easy. We just need to find 312×423 first and then we can find 31.2×42.3.'

a) Here is how she started to find 312×423:

Copy and complete the multiplication grid.

b) What is 312×423?

c) What is 312×42.3?

d) What is 31.2×42.3?

Student's Book exercise 1.2

Use the method from question 31 to find the following:

1 5.2 × 2.4   2 6.3 × 2.6

3 15.1 × 3.6   4 24.6 × 4.2

5 23.7 × 34.3   6 1.25 × 60

Sometimes we may already know a calculation that can help us find another answer. For the next questions use what is given to you to work out each answer.

7 Given that 17 × 18 = 306, what is 1.7 × 1.8?

8 Given that 26 × 35 = 910, what is 0.26 × 3.5?

9 Given that 56 × 42 = 2352, what is 5.6 × 4.2?

10 Given that 56 × 42 = 2352, what is 560 × 0.42?

11 Given that 5.8 × 6.4 = 37.12, what is 58 × 64?

12 Given that 5.8 × 6.4 = 37.12, what is 0.58 × 6.4?

13 Given that 25.1 × 68.3 = 1714.33, what is 2.51 × 0.683?

14 Given that 235 × 0.63 = 148.05, what is 2.35 × 6.3?

33 Sadie wants to have party poppers at the wedding. She has a budget of £10.00 to spend on them. She finds out that they cost £0.04 (4p) each. She knows that the calculation she should do is 10.00 ÷ 0.04. As usual, her bridesmaid Isabella comes to the rescue.

> 10 ÷ 4 = 2.5
> So 10 ÷ 0.4 = 25
> So 10 ÷ 0.04 = 250
> You will therefore get 250 party poppers.

Explain what Isabella has done.

34 Use Isabella's method for division to work out:

a) 28 ÷ 0.4   b) 1.8 ÷ 0.3   c) 4.8 ÷ 0.02

Buying tickets

35 To thank her for all the help, Sadie takes Isabella and two other friends to a gig by their favourite band, The New York Bicycle Clips. The tickets cost £19.50 each and there's a booking fee of £3.00 per ticket. They use their calculators to work out the cost.

Isabella uses '4 × 19.50 + 4 × 3.00'. Her calculator gives the answer 246.

Sadie adds the £3.00 to £19.50 and gets £22.50. She then works out '4 × 22.50'. Her calculator gives the answer 90.

Maddy works out '4 × 19.50 + 4 × 3.00'. Her calculator gives the answer 90.

a) Which do you think is correct, £246 or £90 (or both)?

b) Isabella tries the calculation without a calculator. She works out:

$1 \times 22.50 = \;\; ; 2 \times 22.50 = \;\; ; 4 \times 22.50 =$

Copy and complete the three multiplications above.

c) Why does Isabella's calculator give the answer 246? (It is not broken.) Can you say what calculations it has done?

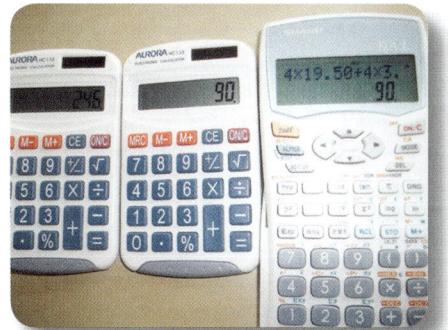

36 Sadie also wants to hire a pink limo to drive them to the gig. It is 16 miles to the gig. The charge for the limo is £50 plus £4 for every mile you travel. They reach for their calculators again and type in '50 + 4 × 16'. Isabella's calculator reads £864, while Maddy's reads £114.

a) Which answer do you think is correct? Why?

b) Work out 50 + 4 × 16 without a calculator.

c) What calculation has Isabella's calculator done to get £864?

37 Maddy's calculator (the one on the right in the photo) is a clever calculator. It knows the rules of mathematics so it will always give the correct answer.

a) When it worked out 50 + 4 × 16, what did it do first, 50 + 4 or 4 × 16?

b) When it worked out 4 × 19.50 + 4 × 3.00, what did it do first, multiply or add?

The rules for calculations

38 So that everyone does each sum in the same way, there are rules for which calculations you should do first. Scientific calculators like Maddy's know these rules.

The rules say you should work out a bracket first, then powers, then division and multiplication, and finally addition and subtraction.

   a) Use the rules to work out $(4 + 3) - 4 \div 2 + 3 \times 3$.

   b) Check your answer using a scientific calculator.

39 Work out the following using the rules:

   a) $4 + 5 \times 6$

   b) $18 - 6 \times 2$

   c) $(18 - 6) \times 2$

   d) $(12 + 8) \div (12 - 7)$

   e) $2 + 16 \div 8 - 4$

40 The rules you have been using are often called BODMAS or BIDMAS. Use the internet to find out why they are called BODMAS or BIDMAS. Write some notes on what you find and do an online search for the BODMAS song!

Summary

The four basic operations we use with numbers are:

addition	+	subtraction	−
multiplication	×	division	÷

A number line can help you make sense of numbers and compare them. It can also help you do calculations.

For **subtraction problems** (such as 436 − 329) you can use these steps:

- Draw a line and place the two numbers on it.
- Make jumps from one number to the other.
- Add all the jumps.

For **multiplication** a tile model can help you break up the problem into easier parts. 23 × 17 can be worked out using a grid like the one on the right:

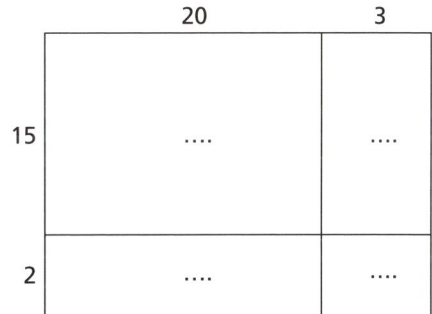

For **multiplication** and **division** problems a ratio table may be useful. This ratio table works out 16 × 24:

Cases	1	10	5	16
Bars	24	240	120	384

Difficult-looking **decimal calculations** can be made easier by multiplying whole numbers first. For example, if you want to find 0.08 × 0.7 you could first work out:

$8 \times 7 = 56$	$8 \times 0.7 = 5.6$
$0.8 \times 0.7 = 0.56$	$0.08 \times 0.7 = 0.056$

If you know an answer to a calculation, you can easily state many other correct calculations. For example, if you know $85 \times 568 = 48\,280$, you also know that:

$850 \times 568 = 482\,800$ and $850 \times 56.8 = 48\,280$ and
$850 \times 5.68 = 4828$ and $850 \times 0.568 = 482.8$ and...

There is a special order for doing calculations if there are lots to do. This is known as **BODMAS/BIDMAS**. To work out $7 + 6 \times 5 - 8 \div 2$ you would do it in this order:

- $6 \times 5 = 30$ and $8 \div 2 = 4$
- This leaves $7 + 30 - 4$
- $7 + 30 - 4 = 33$

(So you do multiplication and division before addition and subtraction.)

Measuring instruments

1 Measuring is part of everyday life. For example, you may set an alarm to wake you up, a teacher might give you 8 out of 10 for your homework, a chef might measure out two cups of water for each cup of rice, or you might hear somebody say, 'I put 2lbs on over Christmas' or, 'My, you are getting tall.' Sometimes the measure is very precise and at other times it's a rough guess or estimate.

On a copy of the table below, write as many measurement units as you know. Also write down what each unit can be used for and what you could use to measure it. Add as many rows as you need to.

Measurement unit	Used to measure (one example)	Measuring instrument used
second	100 metre run	
teaspoon	medicine	

2 Did you mention the unit *stones* to measure your weight? Stones are sometimes used in the UK. Most other European countries use kilograms and grams.

a) Write down the weight of the person shown in this photograph. Make sure you write down the unit.

b) Do you think this person weighs more or less than 10 stones? (One stone is roughly 6.5 kilograms.)

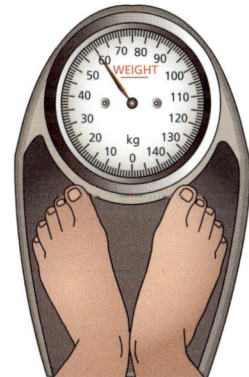

Turn to pages 8–9 of your workbook and read the scales on a variety of measuring instruments shown in Workbook exercise 2.1. Be as precise as possible.

3 This thermometer is also shown in **Workbook exercise 2.1**. In that exercise you wrote down the temperature the pointer indicates.

During the day, the temperature rose by 3 degrees.

a) What will the new temperature be?

b) How is a thermometer similar to a number line?

c) How is it different?

Ten thousand steps a day

4 Health experts tell us, 'Take 10 000 steps a day to lead a healthy life.' What distance do you think you would cover if you walked 10 000 steps?

5 You will probably lose count if you try to count all the steps you take during a day. Instead a **pedometer** may be used, which counts the number of steps you take.

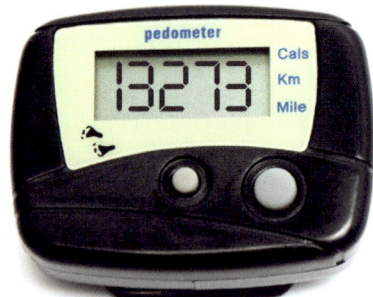

Fouad used the pedometer on the right. Did he take 10 000 steps on that day?

6 Martin and Fouad used the same type of pedometer. Both pedometers were set to zero when they started using them on a hike. By the end of the hike, Fouad's pedometer showed 13 273 steps while Martin's showed 13 914 steps.

Why do you think the two pedometers did not show the same number of steps after the same hike?

7 Different people have different step lengths. This picture shows what a step length is:

Think of a method you could use to find your own step length. Use centimetres (cm) as the unit of measurement to measure your step length.

8 **a)** How many metres do you cover if you take 10 000 steps?
   b) How many kilometres do you cover if you take 10 000 steps?
   c) Did you make a good estimate in **question 5**?

Complete the extra problems about measurements in Workbook exercise 2.2 on pages 10–11 of your workbook.

Height

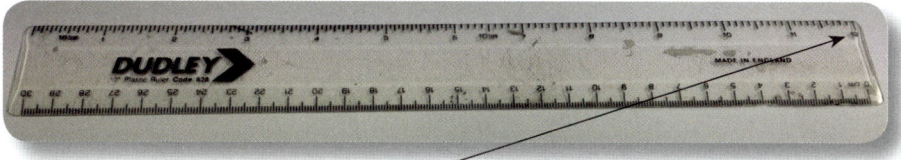

1 foot is 12 inches

9 Looking at the ruler, what do you think 12 inches is in centimetres? This is only an approximate conversion but often a good 'rule of thumb'.

Molly drew the following double number line to represent the ruler.

```
0                                                          30 cm
+-----------------------------------------------------------+
0                                                          12 in
```

a) Make a copy of this number line and mark four other points on it that you know in both centimetres and inches.

b) Roughly how many rulers would you need to put end to end to make a metre?

10 Mark is 5 feet and 3 inches. Alexandra is 1 metre and 72 centimetres. Use the 30 cm to 12 inches rule of thumb to decide who is the taller of the two.

11 A problem when you extend the number line is that it becomes rather difficult to fit on a page. Some people use a ratio table as a more flexible version of a number line. The idea is that you can now fill in other values.

cm		30			
in		12			

a) Look at the following example of a student having partly filled in a ratio table for the ruler. Can you work out how this was done?

cm	15	30	45		
in	6	12	18		

b) The following ratio table was used to work out what 5 ft 3 inches is in centimetres. Can you make sense of it?

cm	7 ½	15	30	60	150	157 ½
in	3	6	12	24	60	63

12 a) Who do you think is the tallest of these celebrities?
- Simon Cowell
- Adele
- Daniel Radcliffe (Harry Potter)
- Wayne Rooney
- Michael Jordan
- Jeremy Clarkson (*Top Gear* presenter)

b) Put them in what you imagine would be their order of height.

Now turn to page 12 of your workbook and do the problems in Workbook exercise 2.3.

13 Blackpool Tower, at 158 m, is barely half the height of the Eiffel Tower (300 m).

Eiffel Tower

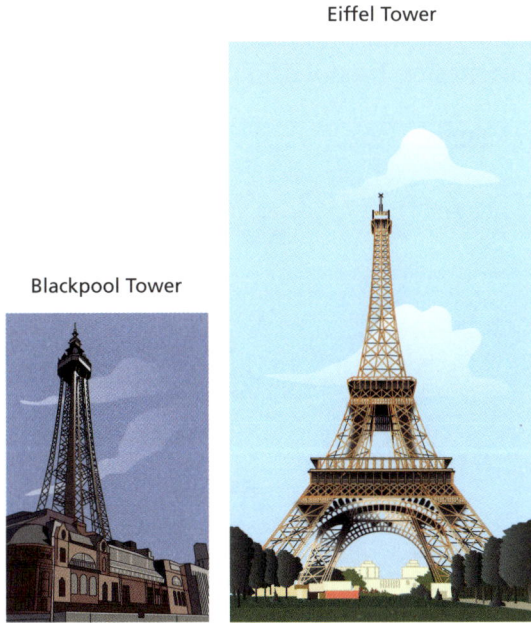

Blackpool Tower

If we used Blackpool Tower as the unit of measurement, the Eiffel Tower would be two Blackpool Towers.

a) The Burj Khalifa building in Dubai is about 830 m high. Roughly how many Blackpool Towers is this?

b) Mount Everest is around 8850 m. Roughly how many Blackpool Towers is this?

c) A metre is approximately 3.3 ft. This means that 3 m is about 10 ft. How tall is the Eiffel Tower in feet?

Motorway routes

14 This map shows part of England and Wales. It shows the main motorway routes in blue. See if you can find the M4, M1 and M6. Look for Birmingham, Manchester, Bristol and Cardiff.

15 Look at the scale in the bottom left-hand corner and use your finger and thumb to get a rough estimate for 50 miles. Use this to estimate the distance between Bristol and Birmingham travelling on the M5.

16 The M25 is the motorway circling London. Can you see it on the map? What do you think the approximate radius is of this motorway?

Try the questions in Workbook exercise 2.4 on pages 13–14 of your workbook.

A real bargain?

17 Marsha lives in St Albans, just north of London. She is going to buy a car in Paris, France. The car is really good value so Marsha doesn't mind spending the money and time travelling to Paris. She has arranged to meet the seller at the train station (Gare du Nord International) in Paris at 5:30pm on Saturday (local time).

The journey will be in two stages:

- Home to London St Pancras, which takes less than 45 minutes by train.
- St Pancras to Paris by train, where she will meet the buyer outside the station.

She will then spend the night near Paris and drive back to England the next day.

Use the map above to help you draw a rough map of southern England and northern France. Show Marsha's journey to Paris on it.

18 Part of a timetable for the journey from London St Pancras to Gare du Nord is shown below.

Departs (Local time)	Arrives (Local time)	Journey time	Standard Great value travel		Standard Premier Enhance your journey		Business Premier For business travellers
			Non flexible	Semi flexible	Non flexible	Semi flexible	Fully flexible
05:40	09:17	02h37m direct	○ £140.00	○ £163.00	○ £123.00	○ £162.00	○ £276.00
07:01	10:17	02h16m direct	○ £140.00	○ £163.00	○ £157.00	○ £188.00	○ £276.00
07:31	10:47	02h16m direct	○ £140.00	○ £163.00	○ £157.00	○ £188.00	○ £276.00
07:54	11:17	02h23m direct	○ £140.00	○ £163.00	○ £157.00	○ £188.00	○ £276.00
08:31	11:47	02h16m direct	○ £140.00	○ £163.00	○ £157.00 less than 10 seats	○ £188.00 less than 10 seats	○ £276.00
09:12	12:47	02h35m direct	○ £140.00 less than 10 seats	○ £163.00 less than 10 seats	○ £157.00	○ £188.00	○ £276.00
10:24	13:47	02h23m direct	Sold out	○ £179.00	○ £192.00	○ £200.00	○ £276.00
12:24	15:47	02h23m direct	Sold out	○ £179.00	○ £192.00	○ £200.00	○ £276.00
14:01	17:17	02h16m direct	Sold out	○ £179.00	○ £192.00	○ £200.00	○ £276.00
15:01	18:17	02h16m direct	○ £140.00 less than 10 seats	○ £163.00 less than 10 seats	○ £157.00	○ £188.00	○ £276.00
16:01	19:17	02h16m direct	○ £140.00 less than 10 seats	○ £163.00 less than 10 seats	○ £157.00	○ £188.00	○ £276.00
16:22	19:47	02h25m direct	○ £140.00	○ £163.00	○ £157.00	○ £188.00	○ £276.00

a) Find on the timetable the train that leaves St Pancras at 10:24. What time does this train arrive in Paris?

b) How long does the journey take?

c) Work out the difference between the start and end time for the journey. Can you explain why it is not the same as the journey time?

d) How much will a semi flexible standard ticket cost on this train?

19 What time do you think Marsha will need to leave home? Explain your reasoning.

20 After buying the car and staying the Saturday night in a town north of Paris called Beauvais, Marsha intends to drive to Calais to get the ferry to Folkestone.

She needs to be at Calais at 12:00 noon.

a) Can you find Beauvais on the map on page 25? (It is around 40 km north of Paris.) About how far is it from Beauvais to Calais?

b) If she averages around 60 km per hour, what time do you think Marsha should leave Beauvais to get to Calais by 12:00?

21 The ferry leaves at 1:00pm local time and takes about 1 hour. Marsha intends to travel from Folkestone by motorway back to St Albans. The route she intends to take is: M20 towards London, M25 anticlockwise and finally the A1081 to St Albans.

a) Make sure you can see her journey on the map below. (You will not be able to see the last part of the journey on this map.)

b) Cars generally average around 60 mph on motorways in England. How long do you think her journey will take?

c) When do you think she will arrive home?

d) What is likely to be the slowest part of her journey?

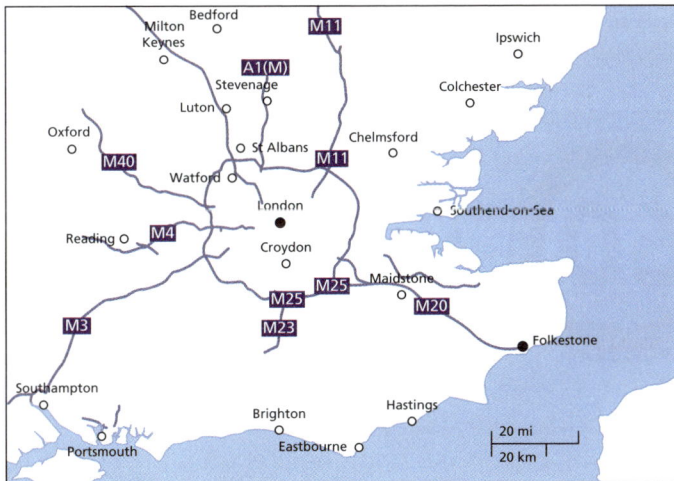

Watch your speed!

22 Marsha bought her new car in France and brought it back to England. The picture shows the speedometer. What do you notice about the speedometer?

23 As Marsha got off the ferry in Folkestone, she quickly realised that she needed to work out the speed in miles per hour (mph) so that she could be sure to stay within the speed limit.

Marsha knows that 50 mph is the same as 80 kilometres per hour.

Look at the British speed limit signs above and try to work out what these are in kilometres per hour. Be prepared to explain how you did the calculations. You can use a ratio table like the one below if it helps.

km/h			80		
mph			50		

24 When Marsha got home she looked at the speedometer in a friend's car (see photo). She could see how useful a dual speedometer could be if you are moving between countries.

Marsha also remembered seeing some very old cars with horizontal speedometers like the one below. This gave her an idea to help her with the conversions.

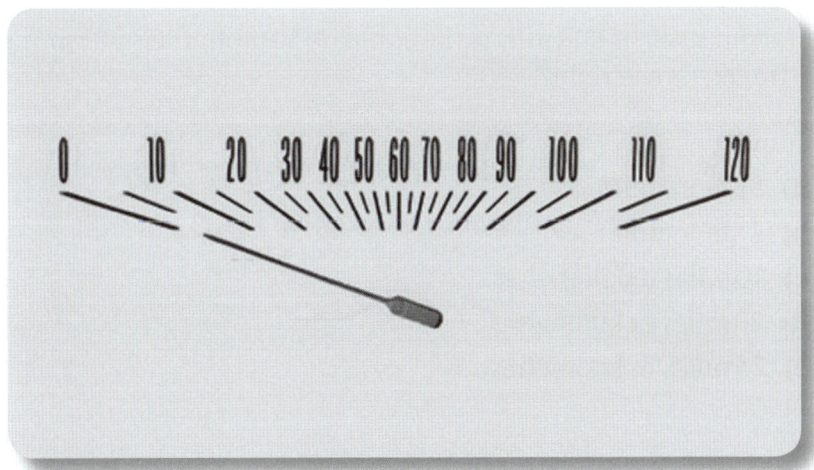

Marsha decided to make a double number line to stick at the bottom of her speedometer. Copy the number line below and mark some easy-to-see speeds on it. Include some speeds greater than 50 mph. Check to see if these match the dual speedometer above.

0 mph   50 mph

0 km/h   80 km/h

25 a) Use your number line from **question 24** to find approximate speeds in mph (to the nearest 5 mph) for the speed limits below.

80 km/h   **120** km/h   **60** km/h

b) Use the number line to find the approximate speeds in km/h for the mph speed limits below.

50   **30**   **10**

26 What is 70 mph in km/h?

27 Marsha says: 'If 80 km/h is the same as 50 mph, then 80 km is the same as 50 miles.' Is she right?

28 Convert:

a) 8 km to miles

b) 4 km to miles

c) 10 miles to kilometres

d) 20 miles to kilometres

e) 25 miles to kilometres

Weighing it up

29 Some countries measure weight using imperial units (pounds, ounces, stones, etc). Other countries use metric units (kilograms, grams, tonnes, etc). Some countries put the equivalent weight in brackets after the unit they normally use and others do not.

a) When the weight is printed on a package, it refers to the net weight rather than the gross weight. Can you explain the difference?

b) Find out which units are usually used in England, France, Spain and the USA.

30 One of the two lists of ingredients for bread below is from the USA. The other is from the UK. Can you tell which is which? Explain your answer.

Pumpkin bread *(about 24 servings)*	**Basic white bread** *(This serves about 12 people)*
4 cups all-purpose flour	1 kg strong bread flour
1 tablespoon baking powder	625 ml tepid water
2 teaspoons ground ginger	30 g fresh yeast or 3 × 7 g sachets dried yeast
1 teaspoon *each*: baking soda, salt, ground cinnamon	2 tablespoons sugar
½ teaspoon ground cloves	1 level tablespoon fine sea salt
4 large eggs, beaten	extra flour for dusting
1½ cups granulated sugar	
1 cup light brown sugar	
2 sticks (1 cup) butter, melted	
1 can (16 ounces) pure pumpkin	

31 Americans use the cup as a measure in many of their recipes. Both the USA and UK use the tablespoon and the teaspoon. Although some people use cups, teaspoons and tablespoons from their kitchen it is possible to buy more precise measures. A teaspoon is 5 ml, a tablespoon is 15 ml and a cup is 240 ml. The stick of butter is an American measure that is the same as 8 tablespoons.

Look at the sets of ingredients in both of the above recipes. Decide which units are measures of volume, which are measures of weight and which are neither.

32 Copy the ratio table below and use it to find how many teaspoons are equal to a cup.

teaspoon	1				?
ml	5				240

33 Copy the ratio table below and use it to find how many tablespoons are equal to a cup.

tablespoon	1				?
ml	15				240

34 The photo shows a box that holds eight half-sticks of butter. It also shows two half-sticks.

a) Can you find three clues that show this box was packed in the USA? What units of weight are used on the packet? What units are used on the half-sticks of butter?

b) Look at the ratio table below. Can you see where the 454 comes from? Copy the table and fill in the next three columns, giving your answer to the nearest whole number. Do your calculations agree with the other information on the half-stick?

Weight in lbs	1	½	¼	⅛		
Weight in grams	454					

35 Look at the ratio table below. Can you see where the first column comes from by looking at the pictures? Copy and complete the table. Can you say what the weight of a carton of butter is in tablespoons?

Weight in tablespoons	4					
Weight in cups	¼	1	2	4	8	

36 Look at the packages below. Try to put them in order of net weight, lowest weight first. Explain how you did this.

37 Look at the four packets in the pictures below. The weights have been hidden. Give a rough estimate of the concealed weights that might be printed on these packets. What order would you put them in, lightest first?

38 The actual weights are shown below. Have a look and see if you were right about the order. What facts are you using to help you decide the order of the weights?

All Purpose Flour: 1 kg

Florida Crystals: 32 oz or 2 lb (907 g)

Special K: 38 oz or 2 lb 6 oz (1.08 kg)

Bran Flakes: 17.3 oz or 1 lb 1.3 oz (490 g)

39 The Special K carton is unusual in that it has two packs inside. How much do you think each of them weighs?

Rounding

40 When working out journeys we often work to the nearest hour, the nearest mile or the nearest 100 miles.

Look at the result from a route planner website shown below. It shows the time and distance from Oldham (near Manchester) to Birmingham.

> **Route results**
>
> **From:** Oldham, Greater Manchester
>
> **To:** Birmingham, West Midlands
>
> **Distance:** 96.3 miles
>
> **Time:** 1 hr 50 min

a) What is the distance between the two places and what is the estimated time for the journey?

b) Birmingham is a very big city so the real distance might be larger or smaller. The time it takes will depend on the time of day you travel. Give a sensible estimate for the real distance and the time for the journey.

41 The journey from Cardiff to Swansea is outlined below. What do you think is the approximate distance and the time needed for this journey?

> **Route results**
>
> **From:** Cardiff, Cardiff
>
> **To:** Swansea, Swansea
>
> **Distance:** 41.6 miles
>
> **Time:** 0 hr 53 min

If you gave 40 miles as your answer we say you have given your answer to the nearest ten. How accurately you give your answer will often depend on the circumstances.

Now turn to pages 15–16 of your workbook and complete Workbook exercise 2.5.

Summary

When measuring objects, it is important to use the correct *unit of measurement*. For conversion purposes, there are rules of thumb (an approximate conversion) as well as formal rules.

Sample rules of thumb:

- 5 miles equals around 8 kilometres or 1 mile is about 1.5 km.
- 1 inch is about 2.5 cm (this works out to be the same as 12 inches equals around 30 cm).
- 1 inch is about the width of a thumb.
- 1 stone is about 6.5 kg.
- 1 kg is about 2.2 lbs (i.e. 1 kg is a little more than 2 lbs).
- 1 m is about 39 inches (so a metre is a little more than a yard).

Sample formal rules:

- 1 foot = 12 inches
- 1 km = 1000 m
- 1 m = 100 cm
- 1 cm = 10 mm
- 1 kg = 1000 g

To convert between units we often use a double number line or a ratio table. For example, the ratio table below is using the rule of thumb conversion that 1 inch is about 2.5 cm to work out the value of 12 inches in centimetres.

inches	1	2	10	12
cm	2.5	5	25	?

Recipes

Pancakes

Serves: Makes 8 pancakes

Ingredients

125 g plain flour, sifted   1 medium egg, beaten

300 ml milk   a little oil for frying

Method

Sift the flour into a bowl and make a well in the centre. Add the egg, then gradually add half the milk, stirring constantly. Add the remaining milk and beat thoroughly, until smooth.

Heat a small omelette pan or frying pan and add a few drops of oil. Pour a little batter into the pan and tilt so that the batter coats the bottom of the pan.

Cook for 1–2 minutes, or until bubbles appear and the underside is golden. Loosen the edges of the pancake, then flip it over and cook the other side for a further 1–2 minutes, or until golden.

Pile the pancakes on to a warm plate, separating them with sheets of greaseproof paper. Keep warm and continue to make 8 pancakes in total.

1 Roughly how long does the recipe suggest it would take to make eight pancakes?

2 Find out if 1 litre of milk is enough to make 24 pancakes. Show your working.

3 There are 28 people in Sue's class and she wants to make pancakes for all of them. Decide how much of each ingredient she will need.

Number of pancakes	8							
Plain flour (g)	125							
Milk (ml)	300							
Eggs	1							

4 Mila plans to make 100 pancakes to sell at the school fair.

   a) Use a ratio table to work out how much milk Mila will need.

   b) If you were shopping for Mila, how much milk would you buy?

Now do Workbook exercise 3.1 on page 17 of your workbook.

5 Mila wants to bake some savoury pancakes with bacon, cheese, ham and mushrooms. To save money, she looks for the 'best buy'.

Here are the options for bacon:

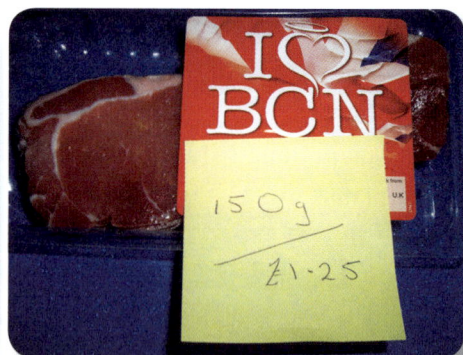

To work out which is the best buy, Mila and Samantha decide to use a ratio table. They begin by doubling to see if this helps them to compare the two buys. After a few minutes, they both have exactly the same thing in their books. This is shown on the right:

Can you decide from here which is the 'best buy'?

g	125	250	500
£	1	2	4

g	150	300	600
£	1·25	2·50	5

6 Mila then does this in her book:

g	125	250	500	625
£	1	2	4	5

g	150	300	600	
£	1·25	2·50	5	

She says: 'So you get more bacon for your money if you buy the 125 g pack.' Discuss with a partner exactly what Mila has done to make this decision.

7 Samantha does it a different way and writes:

g	150	300	600
£	£1.25	£2.50	£5

g	125	250	500	100	600
£	1	2	4	£0.80	£4.80

She says: 'It is cheaper to buy the 125 g pack.'

a) How did Samantha work out that 100 g would cost 80p?

b) Discuss with a partner exactly what she did to be able to compare the two buys.

8 Now use a ratio table to work out the best buy for:

a) Cheese

b) Ham

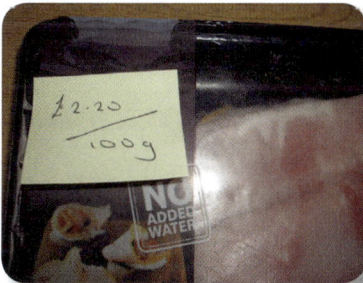 

c) Mushrooms

 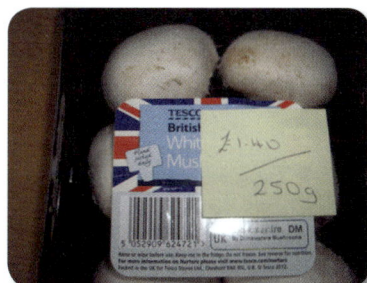

9 Shops often try to help customers decide which the 'best buy' is. Here is part of an online shopping page.

	Nescafe Fine Blend Coffee 100G	**£1.99** (£1.99/100g) Quantity [−] 1 [+] **Add**
	Nescafe Gold Blend Coffee 100G	**£3.28** (£3.28/100g) Quantity [−] 1 [+] **Add**
	Nescafe Gold Blend Coffee 200G	**£6.48** (£3.24/100g) Quantity [−] 1 [+] **Add**
	Nescafe Gold Blend Coffee 300G	**£8.98** (£3.00/100g) Quantity [−] 1 [+] **Add**
	Nescafe Gold Blend Coffee 500G	**£14.90** (£2.98/100g) Quantity [−] 1 [+] **Add**

a) Use the information above to say which of the Nescafe Gold Blend products is the 'best buy'. Explain carefully how you can tell.

b) The 500g tin of coffee costs £14.90. Explain carefully how you could work out that this is £2.98 per 100g.

c) Why do you think shops use the price per 100g to compare prices?

d) Would you usually expect a larger or smaller quantity to be cheaper per 100g? Explain your answer.

e) One of the 'per 100g' costs is an estimate and not an exact amount. Which one is this? Why have they used an estimate in this case?

10 Aimee has started work at the supermarket and has to work out the 100g costs for the website.

Clipper Organic Everyday Tea Bags 160S 500G

Clipper Tea Gold 80'S 250G

PRICE DROP Price Drop Was £2.99 Now £2.00 valid from 16/5/2012 until 12/6/2012

Packers Best Gold Label 80'S Teabags 250G

Packers Best Teabags 160S

> The new price of the tea bags is £2.00 for 250g, but I don't know how to work out the cost of 100g.

Explain carefully how Aimee can work out the cost per 100g. You could use a ratio table to help here.

11 Work out the cost per 100g of the following products, in each case drawing a ratio table to show how you did this.

a) 250g of tea bags priced at £1.50

b) A 400g tin of soup priced at 92p

c) A 1kg box of cornflakes priced at £3.30

d) 750g of cornflakes priced at £2.70

e) A 150g bar of chocolate priced at £1.00

Now do Workbook exercise 3.2 on pages 18–21 of your workbook.

Fuel consumption

12

In order to try and reduce air pollution, drivers are being encouraged to buy cars that are more efficient. One option is to buy a car that travels more miles for every gallon of petrol.

a) Write down three pieces of information that the picture above tells you.

b) What does 34.2 mpg mean in the picture?

13 John sees three cars parked next to each other in the school car park:

- A Citroen C3 1.1i
- A 3.0 Land Rover Range Rover
- A 2.0 Audi TT Coupe (M6)

a) Which car do you think uses the most petrol and why?

b) Which car will use the least petrol?

c) Use the website www.fuel-economy.co.uk to find the fuel consumption figures for each of these cars (click on 'What is my MPG?'). Use this to check your answers to **a)** and **b)**.

d) What do the words 'urban', 'extra-urban' and 'combined' in the website's results mean?

e) Why is the 'urban' figure always the lowest?

f) Each of the cars goes on a journey of 100 miles. Use the 'combined' figures to work out roughly how much petrol each car will use.

g) If petrol is £5.25 per gallon, roughly how much would a 100 mile journey cost each driver?

14 Mrs Jacques owns the Citroen C3. She says:

> Last week I did 500 miles in my car and used 11 gallons of petrol.

Miles	500						
Gallons	11						

a) Is this more or less than the advertised fuel consumption you found in **question 13**?

b) Why do you think we sometimes use more petrol than the advertised amount? (You could investigate this by looking at the 'Top 10 Tips' on the www.fuel-economy.co.uk website.)

15

> We did 350 miles last weekend in our Ford Focus and used 9 gallons of petrol.

> We did 100 miles in our Renault Scenic and used 2½ gallons.

Use the ratio tables below to work out who had the best fuel consumption figures for the weekend.

Miles	350						
Gallons	9						

Miles	100						
Gallons	2.5						

Speed

16 One factor in how much fuel you use is how fast you drive. It took Sheena 2 hours to travel 81 miles.

Sheena says: 'My average speed was 40.5 miles per hour.'

John says: 'That means you drove at the same speed for the whole journey.'

a) Sheena is correct. Explain how Sheena worked out her average speed.

b) Do you think John is correct as well? Explain your answer.

c) Dave travelled 75 miles from Manchester to Birmingham. He left at 8am and arrived at 9:30am. Use the ratio table below to work out his average speed.

Distance (miles)	75						
Time (hours)	1½						

d) Adil drove from Manchester to Oxford, a journey of 140 miles. He left at 10am and arrived at 1:30pm. Who had the higher average speed, Dave or Adil?

17 On a car website, someone asked: 'What is cruise control in cars?' Below is one of the answers.

> Cruise control keeps the speed of the vehicle constant and once engaged the vehicle will maintain that speed. Cruise control will not and cannot activate brakes to stop or slow the vehicle. It does not aid in the steering of the vehicle. The steering and braking is always the responsibility of the driver. Cruise control is not lane control and again it is the driver's responsibility to maintain their lane. Cruise control cannot see obstacles; therefore it is the driver's responsibility to brake for objects, other vehicles, lights and all manner of obstacles.
>
> IN SHORT, CRUISE CONTROL MAINTAINS THE SPEED YOU SET AND NOTHING ELSE.

a) What do you think are the advantages and disadvantages of having a car with cruise control?

b) What type of drivers are most likely to want cruise control?

c) Sheena set the cruise control to 65 mph and drove from 1pm to 2:30pm.

How far did she travel on this part of her journey?

d) Her fuel consumption was 42 mpg. Roughly how much petrol did she use on the journey?

Now do Workbook exercise 3.3 on page 22 of your workbook.

Mobile phone density

18 **a)** If all the students in your class handed in all the mobile phones they own, how many do you think there would be?

   b) If all the students in your school did this, how many do you think there would be?

19 According to a large European research study, people in Europe have an average of 1.3 mobiles that they regularly use. Marcia reads about this and wonders how someone can own 1.3 mobile phones.

   a) Explain to Marcia what is meant by the following statement: *'On average the Europeans in the survey have 1.3 mobiles that they regularly use.'*

   You may want to use an example to make it clear.

   b) How does 1.3 mobiles per European compare with you and your family?

   c) Look back at your answers to **question 18**. How does 1.3 mobiles per person compare to your class and your school?

20 A newspaper article about mobile phone use in the UK commented:

> A recent poll found that most UK adults have at least one mobile phone, with only the very young and very old not owning one at all.
>
> The average mobile phone owner has an average of 1.8 handsets and this is expected to rise to two mobiles for every person soon.
>
> The rise in ownership is thought to be because more people have one mobile for personal calls and another for work. Increased ownership is also being driven by falling costs. Despite the credit crunch, mobile phone networks are offering increasingly competitive prices.

a) If there are around 40 million phone owners in the UK, roughly how many mobile phones are there in the country altogether?

b) In Spain the ratio is 1.45 mobile phones per person. Does this mean that there are more or less mobile phones in Spain than in the UK? Explain your reasoning.

The European study also included the following information:

In Spain, 1 in 3 people have 2 mobile phones that they use regularly.

c) If Spain has about 45 million inhabitants, how many people have 2 mobile phones?

Now do Workbook exercise 3.4 on pages 23–24 of your workbook.

Summary

This chapter has been all about using ratio tables to solve problems. Some students have said that they can use ratio tables to answer about half of all the 'number' questions on their GCSE papers. They also use them for pie charts and other topics.

For example, here are some prices for two packs of ham.

We can use ratio tables to help decide which pack is the 'best buy'.
We begin with:

Weight (gram)	120			
Price (£)	2.40			

Weight (gram)	100			
Price (£)	2.20			

It may be easiest in this case to try to make the top one a 'whole number of hundreds'. So:

Weight (gram)	120	240	480	600
Price (£)	2.40	4.80	9.60	12.00

Now we can get the second one the same:

Weight (gram)	100	200	400	600
Price (£)	2.20	4.40	8.80	13.20

From which we can see that the 120 g pack is better value and so is the 'best buy'.

The highs and lows on Earth

1 Where do you think these pictures were taken?

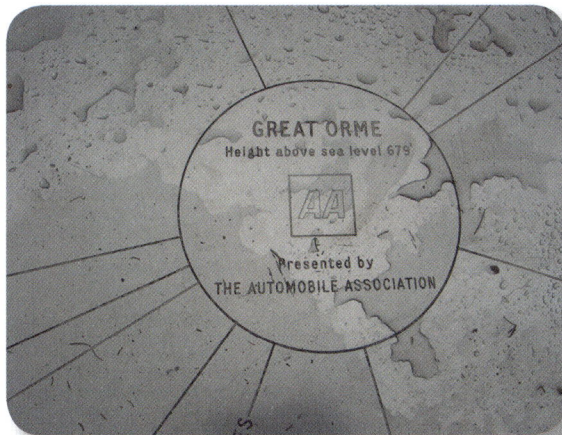

GREAT ORME
Height above sea level 679

AA

Presented by
THE AUTOMOBILE ASSOCIATION

2 Sue and Lorna are discussing a quiz question that asks them where the highest and the lowest points are on Earth. They reckon the highest place is Mount Everest, but argue for a while about where the lowest place can be.

In the end they go on the internet and make a record of some of the places they are interested in. These are shown in the table below:

Place	Lowest point	Highest point
Arctic Ocean	Fram basin −4665 m	Sea level 0 m
Cayman Islands	Caribbean Sea 0 m	The Bluff +43 m
Cooke Islands	Pacific Ocean 0 m	Te Manga +652 m
China	Turpan Pendi −154 m	Mount Everest +8850 m
France	Rhone River delta −2 m	Mont Blanc +4807 m
Iran	Caspian Sea −28 m	Qolleh-ye Damavand +5671 m
Israel	Shore of the Dead Sea −408 m	Har Meron +1208 m
Kenya	Indian Ocean 0 m	Mount Kenya +5199 m
Nepal	Kanchan Kalan +70 m	Mount Everest +8850 m
Pacific Ocean	Mariana Trench −10 924 m	Sea level 0 m
Spain	Atlantic Ocean 0 m	Pico de Teide (Canary Islands) +3718 m
UK	Fenland −4 m	Ben Nevis +1343 m
US	Death Valley −86 m	Mount McKinley +6194 m

a) Write down some things that surprise you when you look at this table.

b) Sue and Lorna did include the highest and the lowest places on Earth in their table. Where are these places?

c) Below are some of the questions Sue and Lorna asked each other when making the table. See whether you can help them.

- 'Mount Everest is given as the highest place in two countries. How can that be the case?'
- 'I suppose it makes sense that the highest point of an ocean would be 0 m?'
- 'How can the Dead Sea be below sea level?'
- 'The highest place I have been to is the Great Orme in North Wales. It's about 200 m high. How many Great Ormes would it take to reach the top of Ben Nevis?'

3 **a)** Which of the places shown above might you choose to go to if you were interested in climbing?

b) Which places shown above might you choose if you wanted to avoid hills and mountains?

c) Of the countries shown in the table, which has the greatest difference in height between the highest and the lowest point?

d) Which country has the least difference in height?

4 Sue wants to get an idea about how the heights of these places relate to each other. She starts to sketch the following:

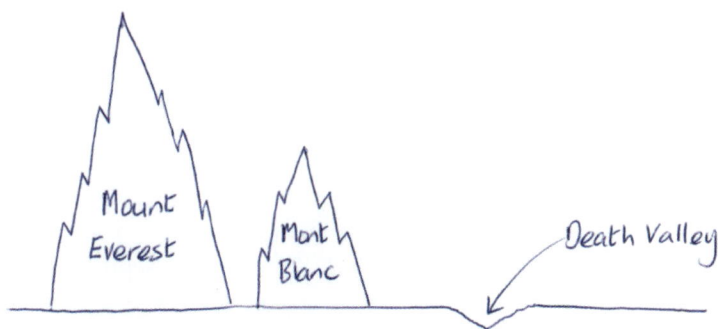

Say whether or not you think she is taking scale into account.

Turn to pages 25–27 of your workbook and do Workbook exercise 4.1.

Time is moving along

5 a) Name some countries that you have been to where you had to change the time on your watch as you got off the plane.

b) Estimate how much adjustment you would need to make if you went to:

   i) New York   **ii)** Sydney

6 Look at the time zone map shown below.

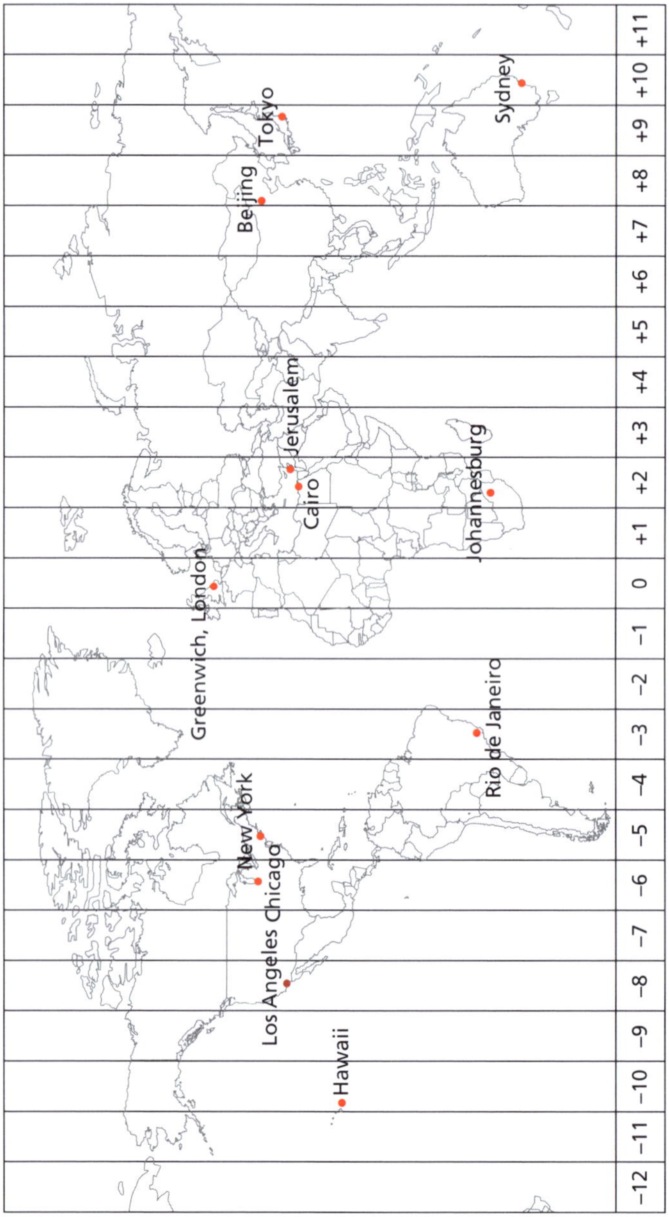

A time zone map can be used to help us calculate the time around the world.

a) If it is 10am in Greenwich, London, what time would it be in Tokyo?

b) When it is midday in Hawaii, where is it midnight?

c) What is the time difference between:
- i) London and New York
- ii) New York and Sydney
- iii) Tokyo and Rio de Janeiro

d) In the 2008 Beijing Olympics, the men's 100 metres sprint took place at 6:30pm local time. At what time would people in the UK have watched this race? What about people in Rio de Janeiro?

e) If you needed to ring a company based in Los Angeles that was open between 9am and 4pm, suggest a sensible time to ring from the UK.

f) Can you think of a situation where you were affected by differing time zones? Describe what happened.

The witch's cauldron

7 Wilhelmina the witch has a magic cauldron in which she can mix a variety of spells. Whether the spell is for good or evil depends upon the temperature of the mixture.

Wilhelmina is able to make the cauldron hotter by adding red cubes and colder by adding blue cubes.

If she adds one red cube this makes the temperature go up by one degree. If she adds one blue cube this makes the temperature go down by one degree.

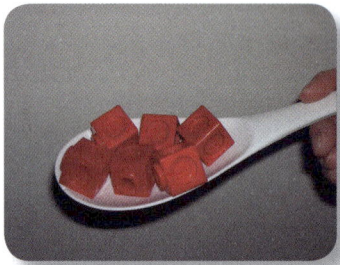

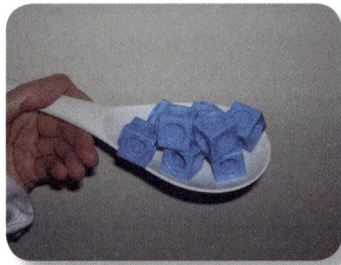

If the temperature of the cauldron is greater then 0°, this will produce a good spell. If the temperature is lower than 0°, this will produce an evil spell. If the temperature is 0°, then the spell has no effect. The cauldron must never be left completely empty or all of its magic powers will be lost forever.

Describe what type of spells will result from a cauldron that contains:

a) 5 blue cubes and 7 red cubes   **b)** 15 blue cubes and 11 red cubes

c) 6 red cubes and 10 blue cubes   **d)** 13 red cubes and 13 blue cubes

8 Wilhelmina puts 2 red cubes in, stirs the mixture and says, 'Hubble, bubble, toil and trouble, this will make the temperature 2 degrees warmer.'

Describe in words what will happen to the temperature if she:

a) puts in 5 red cubes

b) puts in 12 blue cubes

c) puts in 8 blue cubes and then puts in 5 red cubes

d) takes out 6 red cubes

e) takes out 5 blue cubes

f) puts in 3 blue cubes, takes out 7 red cubes, and takes out 2 blue cubes

g) puts in 7 red, takes out 2 blue, then puts in 10 blue and takes out 6 red, and finally puts in 3 blue and puts in 5 red

9 Wilhelmina can't keep track of what she's doing, so she starts to make a record in her witch's notepad.

Notes

$+ {}^+7 - {}^-2 + {}^+10 - {}^+6$

a) Copy down what she has written above for **question 8g)** and finish it off.

b) How many degrees hotter or colder does this make the cauldron?

10 The next day Wilhelmina has this recorded in her notebook:

Notes

$+ {}^+11 + {}^-5 - {}^+7 - {}^-8$

a) She says: 'First I put in 11 red cubes, then I put in…'. Copy and complete her written explanation.

b) How many degrees hotter or colder does this make the cauldron?

11 Wilhelmina decides to keep detailed daily records of what she has done with the mixture and how this affects the temperature. This is what she writes in her notebook for Monday.

Notes

$+ {}^+14 + {}^-17 = -3$

a) Describe what her notes tell you about what she did.

b) What does the −3 mean?

12 Below you can see part of Wilhelmina's notebook for the rest of the week:

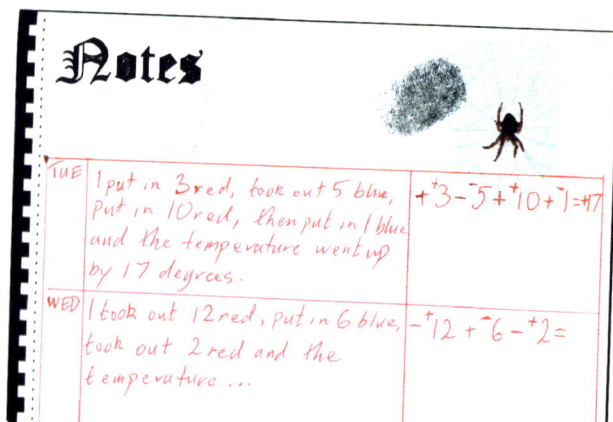

How would the temperature change on Wednesday?

Now turn to pages 28–29 of your workbook and complete Workbook exercise 4.2.

13 Wilhelmina's younger sister Winona comes to stay. Winona is also a witch and she too keeps a record of all her spell mixing. But instead of handwriting her spell book, Winona uses a typewriter.

Winona laughs at how complicated some of her sister's spells look.

'Look at this one,' says Winona, pointing to:

'You don't need to bother with all those extra + signs for red cubes. We witches know what you mean without them. For that spell, I would just type:'

$$6 + - 3 - 7 + 10 = 6$$

Wilhelmina has to agree that this looks less complicated. But she's worried that it might not be clear what you need to do to mix the spell.

What do you think the typed version means in terms of spell mixing?

14 Winona sets her sister a challenge: 'I will type up some spells. You write down what you think they mean and what effect they will have on the temperature.'

Here are the first two spells that she typed up:

Spell	Symbols	Description and temperature change
a.	12+-8=4	I put in 12 red cubes, then put in 8 blue cubes and the temperature went up by 4 degrees
b.	–7+-5+10=	

Of course, Winona wants to check her sister's answers. Then the arguments start.

For spell **b.** (–7 + –5 + 10), Wilhelmina thinks it means: 'Put in 7 blue cubes, put in 5 blue cubes, put in 10 red cubes.'

Winona says it means: 'Take out 7 red cubes, put in 5 blue cubes, put in 10 red cubes.'

So, actually, they only disagree on the meaning of –7 at the start.

a) What do you think the –7 means at the start?

b) Does it matter which way you think of it?

Turn to page 30 of your workbook and complete Workbook exercise 4.3.

15 a) In your notebook, make up some spells of your own. Write these in a table like the one shown above. For each spell **either** write the symbols **or** write the instructions.

b) Hand this table to your neighbour and ask them to fill in the missing parts.

c) Check that they have done this correctly by marking their work.

16 Whilst looking through Winona's notebook, Wilhelmina notices some spells that look very peculiar to her. Examples of these spells are shown below.

$$-3 \times 4 =$$

$$5 \times -6 =$$

$$-3 \times -6 =$$

a) Copy these spells and write down what you think they mean.

b) Share your ideas with your class.

17 On the next page of the notebook Wilhelmina sees the following table:

Sun	$-3 \times 4 = -12$	I took out 3 spoonfuls with 4 red cubes on each one, So the temperature goes down by 12 degrees.
Mon	$5 \times -6 = -30$	I put in 5 spoonfuls with 6 blue cubes on each one, (like $-6 + -6 + -6 + -6 + -6$) So the temperature goes down by 30 degrees.
Tue	$-3 \times -6 = 18$	I took out 3 spoonfuls with 6 blue cubes on each one, So the temperature goes up by 18 degrees.

See if you agree with the descriptions of the spells.

Turn to page 31 of your workbook and complete Workbook exercise 4.4.

18 **a)** In your notebook, make up some spells of your own like the ones above. For each spell either write the symbols or write the instructions.

b) Hand this to your neighbouring witch and ask them to fill in the missing parts.

c) Check that they have done this correctly by marking their work.

19 On the back page of Winona's notebook, Wilhelmina sees some symbols that make no sense to her whatsoever. They are shown below.

$$15 \div -3$$

$$-15 \div -3$$

$$-15 \div 3$$

a) Brainstorm ideas as a class about what these spells might mean.

Wilhelmina can't work out what the symbols mean. She's forced to ask her 'know-it-all' sister.

'15 divided by –3,' says Winona, 'is me trying to work out how many spoonfuls of 3 blue cubes I need to take out to make the temperature go up by 15 degrees.'

'Oh, that's easy then,' says Wilhelmina. 'You need to take out 5 lots of 3 blue cubes, so –5.'

'And –15 divided by –3,' says Winona, 'is how many spoonfuls of 3 blue cubes do I need to make the temperature go down by 15 degrees?'

'You need to put in 5 lots of 3 blue cubes,' says Wilhelmina, 'so that's +5, or just 5.'

b) What do you think they would say –15 ÷ 3 means?

Turn to page 32 of your workbook and do Workbook exercise 4.5.

Summary

In this chapter you looked at the use of positive and negative numbers in several situations.

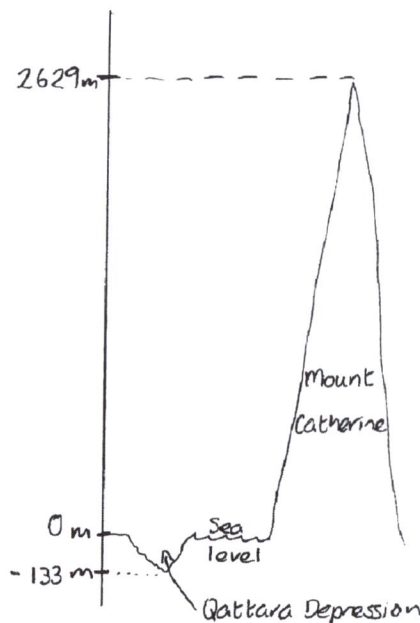

Highest and lowest places on Earth

First you looked at some of the highest and lowest places in the world. Heights are given according to whether they are above or below sea level. A positive distance means the place is above sea level. A negative distance means it is below sea level.

This picture shows the highest and lowest places in Egypt drawn next to a number line. The number line helps you see why the difference in height between the lowest and highest places in Egypt is 2762 m.

Different time zones

Secondly you looked at time differences around the world. A number line like this appears on time zone maps:

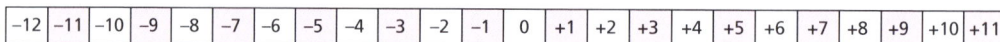

−12	−11	−10	−9	−8	−7	−6	−5	−4	−3	−2	−1	0	+1	+2	+3	+4	+5	+6	+7	+8	+9	+10	+11

This number line helps you to see why the time difference between New York (−5 hours) and Sydney (+10 hours) is 15 hours.

The witch's cauldron

The idea of the witch's cauldron gave you a way to think about problems involving addition and subtraction with negative numbers. For example, −7 − −11 can be thought of as: 'You put in 7 blue cubes and then take out 11 blue cubes, so the temperature will go **up** by 4 degrees.'

So: −7 − −11 = +4 (or you can write this as just 4).

This idea can also help you think about multiplying and dividing with negative numbers. For example, −5 × −4 can be thought of as: 'Take out 5 lots of 4 blue cubes, so the temperature will go **up** by 20 degrees.'

So: −5 × −4 = 20.

12 ÷ −3 can be thought of as: 'How many spoonfuls of 3 blue cubes will I need to make the temperature go up by 12?' Answer: You need to take out 4 spoonfuls.

So: 12 ÷ −3 = −4.

A numbers game

Class activity 1

Playing the numbers game

- Draw a 3 by 3 grid and put a number between 20 and 70 in each square. You are not allowed to use repeats.

- Your teacher will roll two dice. Add together the scores on the two dice.
- If you have a number in your grid that is in the times table of this total then you can cross it off. (If you have more than one number in the times table then you can only cross one of them off.)
- Your teacher will carry on rolling the two dice until one of you has crossed off all your numbers.
- To play the game again, make a new grid and choose some different starting numbers to go in your grid.
- Play the game a few times.

1 a) Write down three examples of numbers that are good to have in your starting grid. Say why they are good numbers for this game.

b) Write down three examples of numbers that you would not recommend other people to put in their starting grid and explain why.

Turn to pages 33–35 of your workbook and do Workbook exercises 5.1 and 5.2.

Using primes to build other numbers

2 Euclid was a Greek mathematician from around 300BC. There are no actual records of when he lived and died, so 300BC is an estimate. Euclid was fascinated by numbers and by shape. He wrote down many of his findings in a book, known as *Euclid's Book of Elements*. Amazingly, part of a version of this book survives to this day. It is kept in the Vatican.

Euclid suggested the idea that you can make every whole number (apart from the number 1) by multiplying prime numbers together. What are your first impressions of this idea?

3 Here are the first few prime numbers:

2, 3, 5, 7, 11, 13, 17, 19, 23, 29, 31, 37...

a) Try to make 21 by multiplying prime numbers together.

b) Now try to make 28 by multiplying prime numbers together.

c) Make as many numbers between 2 and 50 as you can by multiplying prime numbers together.

4 Here are three pupils' attempts to make 48:

Sam:

$$48$$
$$\downarrow$$
$$2 \times 24$$
$$\downarrow$$
$$2 \times 12$$
$$\downarrow$$
$$2 \times 6$$
$$\downarrow$$
$$2 \times 3$$

a) Explain what Sam has done.

b) Where in his work can you see how he made 48?

Max:

$$48 = 2 \times 24$$
$$= 2 \times 2 \times 12$$
$$= 2 \times 2 \times 2 \times 6$$
$$= 2 \times 2 \times 2 \times 2 \times 3$$
$$= 2^4 \times 3$$

c) Explain what Max has done.

d) Where in his work can you see how he made 48?

Molly:

$$48 = 4 \times 12$$
$$2 \times 2 \times 3 \times 4$$
$$2 \times 2 \times 3 \times 2 \times 2$$

e) Explain what Molly has done.

f) Where in her work can you see how she made 48?

5 What happens if you start with 48 = 6 × 8?

6 Look at the following expressions:

$2 \times 2 \times 2 \times 2 \times 3$ $2 \times 3 \times 2 \times 2 \times 2$

$2 \times 2 \times 3 \times 2 \times 2$ $2^4 \times 3$

a) In what ways are these expressions the same and in what ways are they different?

b) Which way of writing the expression do you think is best?

> When you find a way to make a number by multiplying prime numbers together this is called 'Expressing a number as a product of prime numbers'.

7 Express each of the following numbers as a product of prime numbers.

a) 30   **b)** 52   **c)** 60   **d)** 80

e) 100   **f)** 75   **g)** 84   **h)** 105

i) 220   **j)** 113

8 Another student, Aisha, thinks she has a quicker way of finding all the prime factors of a number. This is what she does for 84:

a) What do you think she says in her head when she uses this method?

b) Where are the prime factors of 84 in what she has written?

c) What is 84 written as a product of primes?

d) Use Aisha's method to find all the prime factors of:

     i) 86   **ii)** 40   **iii)** 150   **iv)** 63

     v) 120   **vi)** 48   **vii)** 99   **viii)** 200

```
         84
2  |  42
2  |  21
3  |   7
7  |   1
```

9 Liesel and her brother Joel are playing a game. It involves walking with one foot in front of the other, heel to toe. They both start with their heel on the edge of a flagstone. You score a point the next time your heel exactly lands on the edge of a flagstone.

The flagstones are 80 cm in length. Joel's boots are 15 cm long and Liesel's are 20 cm long.

a) Draw a sketch to show Liesel and Joel taking their first few steps.

b) Investigate whether this is a fair game or not.

c) At what distance from the start line will Liesel and Joel both land with their heel exactly on the edge of the same flagstone?

10 Next, Liesel and Joel invent a similar game with their scooters. They put a sticker to mark the bottom of their scooter wheel. This time they start with the bottom of the wheel on the edge of the flagstone. Again, you score a point when the bottom of the wheel next hits a gridline.

The circumference of Liesel's scooter wheel is 50 cm. Joel's is 30 cm. The flagstones are still 80 cm long.

a) Draw a sketch to show what this game looks like.

b) Who is most likely to win this game?

11 Liesel decides to change her scooter for her bike. The circumference of her bike wheel is 120 cm.

a) Does this improve her chances of winning or not? Explain.

b) Suggest some good sizes of wheel to have in this particular game.

12 While Liesel and Joel are playing out, the doorbell goes. It is the window cleaner. Liesel's mum has just enough money to pay him. She starts to worry that the gardener might also be coming today. The window cleaner cleans on a Wednesday once a fortnight. The gardener comes once every 20 days (including on Saturdays and Sundays).

The picture shows a snapshot of the family calendar:

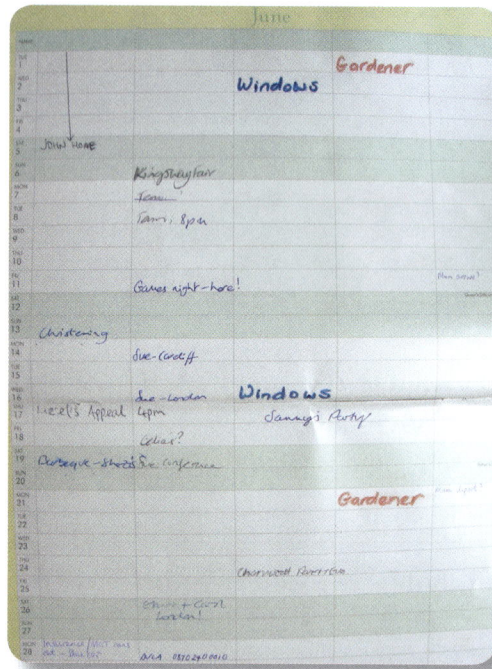

On how many days during a year would you expect both the gardener and the window cleaner to come on exactly the same day?

13 Liesel's mum is baking cakes for Liesel's birthday party. In order to make sure there is enough cake to go in every guest's party bag, she is making two cakes. The chocolate cake ends up weighing 390 grams, while the teddy cake is nearer 180 grams.

Liesel's mum would like to cut the cakes up so that each piece is equal in weight and no cake is left over.

If you do this, what is the biggest weight you could have for each piece?

Packing boxes

14 The building blocks shown below can be ordered in various quantities. The cubes are packaged in boxes ready for distribution.

a) One of the boxes holds 24 cubes. What could be the dimensions of this box?

b) Could a box holding 30 cubes have the same height as the box holding 24 cubes? Explain.

c) The box designers would like their boxes to stack exactly on top of each other. This would require the base of each box to have exactly the same length and width. Is it possible for the box holding 24 cubes to stack exactly on top of the box holding 30 cubes? If so, how can it be done?

15 The cubes shown below are commonly used in schools. They can be ordered in three different amounts. The small box holds 250 cubes, the medium box holds 450 cubes and the large box holds 700 cubes.

The company manufacturing the cubes would like their boxes to stack exactly on top of each other. This would require the base of each box to have the same length and width.

Suggest some possible dimensions for each of the three box sizes.

Finding the highest common factor

16 A group of students were asked to find the highest common factor of 36 and 60. The students used a variety of methods. Here are three examples:

Karen

㊱36

1×36	1×60
2×18	2×30
3×12	3×20
4×9	4×15
6×6	5×12
~~$9 \times$~~	6×10

㊱60

HCF is 12

Mariam

$$\begin{array}{r|r} & 36 \\ \hline 2 & 18 \\ 2 & 9 \\ 3 & 3 \\ 3 & 1 \end{array} \qquad \begin{array}{r|r} & 60 \\ \hline 2 & 30 \\ 2 & 15 \\ 3 & 5 \\ 5 & 1 \end{array}$$

Hcf is $2 \times 2 \times 3 = 12$

Saeed

$36 = 6 \times 6$ $60 = 6 \times 10$
      $= 2 \times 3 \times 2 \times 3$ $= 2 \times 3 \times 5 \times 2$

HCF is $2 \times 3 \times 2 = 12$

a) Why do you think they chose 12 as the highest common factor of 36 and 60?

b) Saeed has written 36 as $2 \times 3 \times 2 \times 3$. Karen has written 36 in factor pairs. Where can you see each of Karen's factor pairs, such as 2×18, in the version $2 \times 3 \times 2 \times 3$ that Saeed has used?

c) Use Karen's, Saeed's and Mariam's methods to find the HCF of:

   i) 28 and 70   **ii)** 45 and 60

d) Describe each person's method for finding the HCF.

e) Use a method of your choice to find the HCF of:

   i) 28 and 42   **ii)** 32 and 80   **iii)** 36 and 84

   iv) 40 and 100   **v)** 34 and 68   **vi)** 75 and 300

Finding the lowest common multiple

Turn to your workbook and complete Workbook exercise 5.3 on pages 36–39.

17 A group of students were asked to find the lowest common multiple of 18 and 60. Here are some of the methods they used:

Karen

18	60
36	120
54	⟨180⟩
72	
90	
108	
126	LCM of 18 and 60 is 180
144	
162	
⟨180⟩	

Saeed

$18 = 3 \times 6$ $60 = 6 \times 10$
$\quad = 3 \times 2 \times 3$ $\quad = 2 \times 3 \times 5 \times 2$

I need 2×2 if the 2's will go into it
I need 3×3 if the 3's will go into it
I need 5 if the 5 will go into it

So LCM $= 2 \times 2 \times 3 \times 3 \times 5$
$\qquad\qquad = 180$

Mariam

18		60	
2	9	2	30
3	3	3	10
3	1	2	5
		5	1

I need a multiple of 60
that 18 will go into.
So I need 2×2× 3×5 for 60
and I need to × 3 so 18 will fit in.

Lcm is $(2 \times 2 \times 3 \times 5) \times 3$
$\qquad = 180$

a) Why do you think 180 is given as the lowest common multiple of 18 and 60?

b) Use each person's method to find the lowest common multiple of:
   i) 15 and 20   **ii)** 12 and 45

c) Describe each person's method for finding the LCM.

d) Use a method of your choice to find the lowest common multiple of:
   i) 14 and 40   **ii)** 9 and 15   **iii)** 16 and 36
   iv) 30 and 120   **v)** 42 and 70   **vi)** 75 and 90
   vii) 56 and 88   **viii)** 64 and 100

Summary

Expressing a number as a product of prime numbers

In this chapter you looked at Euclid's idea that all numbers can be made by multiplying prime numbers together. This turned out to be true (unless the number was itself already a prime).

So, for example:

$80 = 8 \times 10$ (8 and 10 are not prime, so you find a way to make them using primes)

i.e. $80 = 8 \times 10$

$= (2 \times 4) \times (2 \times 5)$ (which is fine apart from the 4, so replace it with 2×2)

$= (2 \times 2 \times 2) \times (2 \times 5)$ (check that this does actually make 80)

$= 2^4 \times 5$

We say that 80 expressed as a product of primes is $2^4 \times 5$

Why do you think that the prime numbers are often referred to as the building blocks of numbers?

You also looked at various methods for finding the highest common factor and the lowest common multiple.

Finding the highest common factor

The highest common factor of 36 and 80 means we are looking for a number that is both a factor of 36 and a factor of 80. There may be several factors in common to both numbers, but we want the highest one.

Look back at the various methods used in this chapter to find the highest common factor and decide which would be your preferred method for finding the HCF of 36 and 80.

Finding the lowest common multiple

The lowest common multiple of 36 and 80 means we are looking for a number that is both a multiple of 36 and a multiple of 80. There are lots of common multiples, but we want the lowest one.

Look back at the various methods used in this chapter to find the lowest common multiple and decide which would be your preferred method for finding the LCM of 36 and 80.

Writing big numbers

1 **a)** Write the number in the picture on the right in words.

   b) What is the message in this picture?

1,500,000
PEOPLE OWN A PIECE OF THIS CAMPAIGN

Supporters like you have built the largest grassroots movement in the history of presidential politics.

DONATE NOW

2 **a)** Write down a big number.

   b) Compare your number with your neighbour. Whose is the biggest?

   c) Write down a *really* big number. Now try to say it.

   d) Compare your number with the rest of your class. Whose is the biggest?

   e) Now try to write down a bigger number than anyone else in the class.

   f) Whose was the biggest? How long did it take you to write it?

   g) Everyone try to write a bigger number than this, even your teacher.

   h) Could anyone do this quickly?

3 Write the following as numbers:

   a) One thousand

   b) Ten thousand

   c) One hundred thousand

   d) One million

   e) Ten million

4 This is a photo of some US dollars.
   Estimate how many dollars there are in this picture.

Writing mathematically – power notation

> You may remember that $5 \times 5 = 5^2$ ('five squared' or 'five to the power of two') and $10 \times 10 = 10^2$ ('ten squared' or 'ten to the power of two').

We can also write numbers with other **powers**. For example:
$1000 = 10 \times 10 \times 10 = 10^3$ and
$1\,000\,000 = 10 \times 10 \times 10 \times 10 \times 10 \times 10 = 10^6$

5 Write the following numbers using power notation:

a) 10 000   **b)** 100 000   **c)** 1 000 000 000 000

> We have just seen that $1\,000\,000 = 10^6$ (one million). We could write $2\,000\,000$ as 2×10^6 (two million). We say that numbers written like this are in **standard form**.

6 Harry's teacher said he had a quick way of writing big numbers. He wrote:

$$1.5 \times 10^{14}$$

Harry didn't think this looked like a very big number at all.

a) Do you think that this is a big number?

b) Is this number bigger than a million?

c) What do you think this number would look like without the power in it?

d) Discuss your ideas with your neighbour.

7 a) How many millimetres do you think it is to the Sun?

b) There are approximately 1.5×10^{14} millimetres to the Sun. $1.5 \times 10^{14} = 150\,000\,000\,000\,000$. Why do you think we sometimes write numbers of this size with powers in them?

c) What does 10^{14} mean?

d) Copy and complete:
$10^{14} = 10 \times 10 \times 10 \times \ldots\ldots\ldots\ldots \times 10$
$= 1000\ldots\ldots\ldots 0$

Turn to page 40 in your workbook and complete Workbook exercise 6.1.

Big cities?

8

a) About 1 000 000 people live in Birmingham. Write this number in power form.

b) About 7 000 000 people live in London. How many times more people live in London than in Birmingham?

c) Explain why the number of people living in London can be written like this:

7×10^6

*(Hint: Look at your answers to parts **a)** and **b)**.)*

d) The number of people who live in Liverpool is 5×10^5. What is this number written in the normal way?

e) The number of people who live in Karachi (Pakistan) is 9×10^6. What is this number written in the normal way?

f) The number of people who live in Lahore (Pakistan) is 5×10^6. Do more people live in Lahore or Karachi? Is it a lot more or only a few more?

g) Write 5×10^6 in the normal way.

A strange reward?

There was once a doctor a long time ago who cured the King's dying son. The King was so happy that he offered the doctor any reward he wanted. The doctor thought for a while and then pointed to a chessboard. He said for his reward he would have one grain of rice on the first square, two grains of rice on the second square, four grains of rice on the third square, eight grains of rice on the forth square, and so on, each square having twice as many grains as the square before.

9 Do you think this was a good reward or not? Why?

10 Sophie thinks she will try to decide if this was a good reward by putting grains of rice on a chessboard in her classroom. She has got up to square 8.

a) How much rice will there be on square 5?

b) How much rice will there be on square 6? How did you find your answer?

c) Can you see any problems Sophie might have as she moves on to squares 6, 7, 8 and so on?

Sophie gives up putting rice on the board and just writes down the number of grains on each square. Turn to page 41 in your workbook and use Workbook exercise 6.2 to record the number of grains on the first 20 squares.

11 a) What do you multiply by to get from the number on one square to the number on the next square?

b) What do you do to go back to the number on the square before?

c) What do you multiply by to move forward two squares? Three squares? Four squares?

12 Use your answers to **Workbook exercise 6.2** to answer the following:

a) $16 \times 2 =$ **b)** $8 \times 2 =$ **c)** $512 \times 2 =$

d) $32 \times 2 =$ **e)** $16 \times 2 \times 2 =$ **f)** $2 \times 2 \times 2 =$

g) $2 \times 2 =$ **h)** $2 \times 2 \times 2 \times 2 =$

13 Sophie thinks she could write all the numbers of grains of rice by multiplying 2s together. For example, $32 = 2 \times 2 \times 2 \times 2 \times 2$. Do you think she could do all the others? How do you know?

14 $2 \times 2 \times 2 \times 2 \times 2$ can be written as 2^5 (2 to the power of 5). You should have 128 in the bottom right-hand corner of **Workbook exercise 6.2**. Write this as a power of 2.

Turn to page 42 of your workbook. Inside each square of the board in Workbook exercise 6.3, write down the number of grains of rice using power notation.

15 How does writing numbers using power notation make things easier? What is the benefit?

16 a) How much rice would there be on the last square of the chessboard?

b) Make a guess as to how many 1 kg bags this would fill.

c) Guess how much 1 kg of rice would cost.

d) Have you changed your mind about whether the doctor's choice is a good reward or not? (*Even if you don't like rice, you could sell it on eBay!*)

17 When Sophie was doing **question 11**, she noticed that the numbers she multiplied with to move forward one square, two squares, three squares, etc. were all powers of 2 (2, 4, 8, 16...).

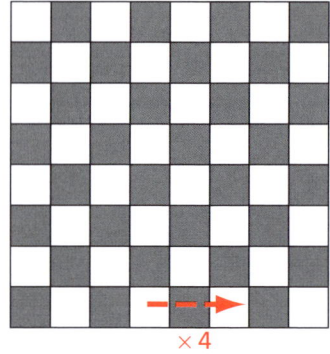

×4

a) To move two squares forward we multiplied by 4. Write 4 as a power of 2.

b) To move three squares forward we multiplied by 8. Write 8 as a power of 2.

c) To move four squares forward we multiplied by 16. Write 16 as a power of 2.

d) Use your answers and the square from **Workbook exercise 6.3** to explain why the following is true: $2^3 \times 2^2 = 2^5$

e) Use your answers and the square from **Workbook exercise 6.3** to explain why the following is true: $2^5 \times 2^3 = 2^8$

f) What is $2^{16} \times 2^4$?

g) What is $2^{101} \times 2^{15}$?

18 a) Is this correct: $3^2 \times 3^3 = 3^5$? How do you know?

b) Is this correct: $10^2 \times 10^1 = 10^3$? How do you know?

c) What is $10^{24} \times 10^{41}$?

Index laws for multiplication:

You will have noticed that $10^5 \times 10^6 = 10^{(5+6)}$.
This is true for any number,
so $x^a \times x^b = x^{(a+b)}$.

---

19 **a)** Look again at your chessboards from **Workbook exercises 6.2** and **6.3**.

     i) What is happening when you move one square to the left?

     ii) What about moving two squares to the left?

     iii) What do you think the answer is to: $2^6 \div 2^2$?

  b) Is this correct: $2^{11} \div 2^3 = 2^8$?

  c) Is this correct: $10^5 \div 10^2 = 10^3$? (*Use your calculator if you want to.*)

  d) What do you think $x^a \div x^b$ equals? (*This is the index law for division.*)

Turn to page 43 in your workbook and complete Workbook exercise 6.4.

20 Sophie heard another strange story that she thought was similar to the chessboard one. It was about a billionaire who offered his son a choice of birthday presents:

Option 1: £1 000 000 on his birthday.

Option 2: 1p on the first day of the month, 2p on the second day of the month, 4p on the third day of the month, 8p on the fourth day of the month, 16p on the fifth day of the month… all the way to the last day of the month.

  a) Which option would you choose?

  b) Which option would give you more money? How much more?

Problems with tiling

21 Bert and Ernie are repairing some tiling on a swimming pool. The area that they need to fix is $2\,m^2$. The small blue tiles that they use each have an area of $1\,cm^2$. They want to know how many tiles they will need.

Bert says: 'There are 100 cm in 1 m so there must be $100\,cm^2$ in $1\,m^2$. We need to fix $2\,m^2$ so we will need 200 small blue tiles.'

Ernie says: '200 tiles doesn't seem enough. I think there will be more than $100\,cm^2$ in a square metre.'

Do you agree with Bert or with Ernie?

22 Ernie decides to prove that he's right. He makes a square metre with metre rulers and starts to fill it with $1\,cm^2$ squares. The pictures that follow show what he did.

Look at the three pictures. Ernie has made 11 complete rows and placed the first 10 squares in the 12th row before running out of squares.

a) How many of the small (1 cm²) squares are there in one complete row?

b) How many rows altogether would be needed to fill in the whole square metre?

c) How many small (1 cm²) squares would be needed to fill in the whole square metre?

d) How many 1 cm² are there in 1 m²?

23 How many 1 cm² tiles will Bert and Ernie need in order to repair the 2 m² area of swimming pool?

24 How many 1 mm² are there in 1 cm²? (*Hint: Draw a square centimetre and think about how many rows of 1 mm there would be along one of the sides.*)

25 There are 1000 mm in 1 m. How many 1 mm² will there be in 1 m²?

A special power

26 Look at the picture below.

a) How many green blocks are there in the first cube?

b) How many blue blocks are there in the second cube?

c) How many yellow blocks are there in the third cube?

d) Describe what the fourth cube would look like (don't worry about the colour!).

e) How many blocks would you need to make the fourth cube?

27 Harry and Lucas are making cubes like the ones shown above. Harry wants to make the tenth cube. He wonders how many little cubes he will need.

There will be a lot more than 60. One face of the cube alone will have 100 (10 × 10) cubes.

There are 6 sides to the cube so the tenth cube will be made with 60 (6 × 10) little cubes.

Harry

Lucas

Do you agree with Harry or with Lucas? Explain why.

28 Look at this picture of one side of the tenth cube:

a) How many little cubes are there along one edge?

b) How many little cubes are there on one side/face?

c) Explain why the total number of little cubes in the tenth cube will be 1000 (10 × 10 × 10).

> A special power:
> $4 \times 4 \times 4 = 4^3$. We call this 4 cubed.
> $4^3 = 64$ so 64 is a cubic number.
> $x \times x \times x = x^3$. We call this x cubed.

29 a) Why do you think we call it 'cubed' when it is a number to the power of 3?

b) Work out 2^3.

c) Work out 5 cubed.

30 Which of the following numbers are cubic numbers:

a) 27

b) 36

c) 100

d) 1000

e) 1

Turn to page 44 in your workbook and complete Workbook exercise 6.5.

Summary

Writing numbers using powers

In this chapter you have seen how big numbers can be written in a shorter way using powers. For example, Roman Abramovich, the owner of Chelsea FC, has a personal wealth of £10 000 000 000. This number could be written in a much shorter way as 10^{10}.

($10^{10} = 10 \times 10 \times 10 \times 10 \times 10 \times 10 \times 10 \times 10 \times 10 \times 10 = 10\,000\,000\,000$)

Multiplying and dividing powers

When we looked at the chessboard problem, we found that the numbers of grains of rice on each square were all powers of 2 (1, 2, 4, 8, 16, 32, 64). To move from one square of the chessboard to the next we multiply by 2 and to move forward two squares we multiply by 4 (or 2^2).

Therefore:
$8 \times 4 = 32$ or
$2^3 \times 2^2 = 2^5$

We found that this worked for all numbers and so:

$$x^a \times x^b = x^{(a+b)}$$

We saw that there is a similar rule when moving backwards on the chessboard:
$2^7 \div 2^3 = 2^4$

This led to this similar rule for dividing powers:

$$x^a \div x^b = x^{(a-b)}$$

Square numbers

Any number to the power of 2 is a square number. The first 12 square numbers are: 1, 4, 9, 16, 25, 36, 49, 64, 81, 100, 121, 144.
Think of the sides and area of a square when working out square numbers.

Cubic numbers

Any number to the power of 3 is a cubic number. The first five cubic numbers are: 1, 8, 27, 64, 125.
Think of the sides and volume of a cube when working out cubic numbers.